IT'S TIME TO LEARN ABOUT ANKYLOSAURUSES

It's Time to Learn about Ankylosauruses

Walter the Educator

Silent King Books
A WhichHead Entertainment Imprint

Copyright © 2025 by Walter the Educator

All rights reserved. No part of this book may be reproduced in any manner whatsoever without written per- mission except in the case of brief quotations embodied in critical articles and reviews.

First Printing, 2024

Disclaimer

This book is a literary work; the story is not about specific persons, locations, situations, and/or circumstances unless mentioned in a historical context. Any resemblance to real persons, locations, situations, and/or circumstances is coincidental. This book is for entertainment and informational purposes only. The author and publisher offer this information without warranties expressed or implied. No matter the grounds, neither the author nor the publisher will be accountable for any losses, injuries, or other damages caused by the reader's use of this book. The use of this book acknowledges an understanding and acceptance of this disclaimer.

It's Time to Learn about Ankylosauruses is a collectible early learning book by Walter the Educator suitable for all ages belonging to Walter the Educator's Time to Eat Book Series. Collect more books at WaltertheEducator.com

USE THE EXTRA SPACE TO TAKE NOTES AND DOCUMENT YOUR MEMORIES

ANKYLOSAURUSES

Long ago, in days of old,

It's Time to Learn about
Ankylosauruses

Lived a dino strong and bold.

With armored plates from head to toe,

Ankylosaurus moved so slow.

Its back was covered, thick and wide,

With bony plates on every side.

Like a tank, it marched along,

Big and heavy, tough and strong.

A mighty tail, oh, what a sight!

It had a club to swing and fight.

If danger came, it took a stand,

Swinging hard to guard the land.

It wasn't fierce, it wasn't mean,

It liked to keep the forests green.

Munching plants was what it did,

Eating leaves since it was a kid!

It's Time to Learn about
Ankylosauruses

Its legs were short, its body low,

It couldn't run but it could go.

Step by step, it roamed around,

Stomping softly on the ground.

Tyrannosaurs would roar and chase,

But Ankylosaurus knew its place.

With armor strong and tail so fast,

It made sure it was never last!

In forests lush and rivers wide,

It found good plants and liked to hide.

With colors blending, brown and gray,

It stayed unseen most of the day.

It laid its eggs, so safe and sound,

Then hid them well beneath the ground.

When babies hatched, they soon would grow,

It's Time to Learn about
Ankylosauruses

With tiny plates all in a row.

Though long extinct, we still can find

Its bones and fossils left behind.

From rocks and dirt, we learn and see

How great this dino used to be!

Now you know this ancient tale,

Of a dino tough and pale.

Ankylosaurus, strong and bright,

It's Time to Learn about
Ankylosauruses

A walking tank, what a sight!

ABOUT THE CREATOR

Walter the Educator is one of the pseudonyms for Walter Anderson. Formally educated in Chemistry, Business, and Education, he is an educator, an author, a diverse entrepreneur, and he is the son of a disabled war veteran. "Walter the Educator" shares his time between educating and creating. He holds interests and owns several creative projects that entertain, enlighten, enhance, and educate, hoping to inspire and motivate you. Follow, find new works, and stay up to date with Walter the Educator™ at WaltertheEducator.com

www.ingramcontent.com/pod-product-compliance
Lightning Source LLC
LaVergne TN
LVHW052016060526
838201LV00059B/4061